Hearts *of* Gold

B R O K E N   B O D I E S

Immeasurable

Blessings

Kathy Pounds Graham

CITIOFBOOKS, INC.
3736 Eubank NE Suite A1
Albuquerque, NM 87111-3579
www.citiofbooks.com
Hotline: 1 (877) 389-2759
Fax: 1 (505) 930-7244

Ordering Information:
Quantity sales. Special discounts are available on quantity purchases by corporations, associations, and others. For details, contact the publisher at the address above.

Printed in the United States of America.
ISBN-13:   Paperback   979-8-89391-653-9
               eBook   979-8-89391-655-3
               Hardback   979-8-89391-654-6

Library of Congress Control Number: 2025907697

DEDICATION

**To the Loves of My Life, Shawn and Jason Odle —
affectionately known to many as "The Guys."**

This series, *Hearts of Gold: Broken Bodies,*
Immeasurable Blessings, is lovingly dedicated to
both of you. Your lives brought countless blessings in
ways words can hardly capture. Through this work,
I hope to share the struggles and triumphs we faced
together—to offer encouragement to others and
raise awareness about life with physical and societal
limitations.

It was the greatest honor of my life to be your mother
here on earth. Now, you rest in the loving arms of our
Lord and Savior, Jesus Christ.

Born two years and eight months apart, you were not
only gifts to one another but fierce warriors chosen for
the road ahead. More than that, you were a gift to all
of us—a radiant light illuminating the often-hidden
world of disabilities.

To the individuals and families who bravely defy
social norms, enduring pain and sacrifice in pursuit of
dignity and inclusion: I hope this message resonates
with you and strengthens your commitment to
advocacy. May you be inspired to stand boldly.

This poem is dedicated to Heaven's Special Children,
who bring light, love, and purpose into our lives,
and to the parents and caregivers
who nurture their incredible journeys
with boundless faith and devotion.
A meeting was held quite far from earth.
"It's time again for more births,"
said the angels to our Heavenly Father above.
"These children will be special and need much love.
The progress will be slow,
and accomplishments may not be shown.
Extra care will be required of the folks they meet down there.
They may not laugh and run nor play as the other children.
Their thoughts at times may seem far away.
They will be labeled on human terms as helpless, different, or disabled.
So, we must be careful where they are sent.
We want their lives to be content.

So, Lord, we ask You to find parents
who will do this special job for You.
They will not realize right away
the leading role they are asked to play.
But with these children sent from above
comes stronger faith and richer love.
Soon they will know the privilege given
in caring for their gift from Heaven.
Their precious gift, so meek and mild,
so heart-rendering,
is Heaven's very special child.

Table of Contents

ACKNOWLEDGMENT

Danny and Valerie Buchanan

Billie Norris

North Mississippi Rehabilitation Center

Charlie Brown House

Dr Edward Ivancic

Sue Nell Searcy

LeBonheur Children's Hospital

UMC Children's Rehabilitation Center

To all the therapists, teachers and parents of children with special needs who gave strength and encouragement.

INTRODUCTION

This documentary is a tribute to Shawn Odle and Jason Odle, whose lives radiated love and joy to all who knew them. They devoted their time on earth to making a meaningful impact, showing the world that limitations need not define one's ability to explore life or strive for their highest potential. Their journey was one of unwavering advocacy—for children, for individuals with disabilities, and through their ministry, Glorify Our Amazing Lord.

It wasn't until 1998 that they received an accurate diagnosis: Pelizaeus-Merzbacher disease, a rare degenerative disorder that affects the myelin sheath in the brain. Doctors once predicted they wouldn't live into their teenage years. Yet, Jason lived to be 45, and Shawn to 47—defying every expectation.

This documentary tells their powerful story—one of courage, perseverance, and living life to its fullest against all odds.

CHAPTER 1

ROOTS OF FAITH AND FAMILY

My life, both simple and complex, began with deep roots in the quiet countryside of northeast Mississippi. I was born into a hardworking farm family, surrounded by the values of faith, family, and community. From an early age, I was blessed to be introduced to church life by our neighbors—people who soon became my spiritual family.

I learned to sing hymns beneath a quilting frame while my spiritual mothers quilted and sang His praises. It was a beautiful, sacred experience that shaped my heart. Before long, my entire family was attending that little church on the hill—a church that would become a cornerstone in my life. It was there I would be baptized, later married, and eventually bring my own children to worship.

Motherhood became one of the greatest blessings of my life. I married in July 1972, and was overjoyed with the births of my two sons, Shawn and Jason.

Shawn, my firstborn, was born on October 4, 1974, weighing 7 pounds 2 ounces and measuring 19 inches long. From the beginning, he was a bundle of joy—always happy and eager to connect with people.

Though his development was slower than expected, every milestone he reached was a cause for celebration and gratitude.

Then God sent Jason our way.

Jason was born on June 15, 1977, weighing 7 pounds 6 ounces and measuring 18 inches. He was muscular and strong, with no signs of any health concerns. Like his brother, he was a joyful baby, though a bit more fussy than Shawn. He, too, loved being around people and engaging with the world.

Shawn adored his baby brother from the start. He would lie next to Jason on the blanket for hours, playing and watching over him. If Jason so much as whimpered, Shawn would cry out for us in concern.

We often said that God sent Jason to be Shawn's companion on this journey through life. Though their challenges would be similar in some ways, each would face them differently.

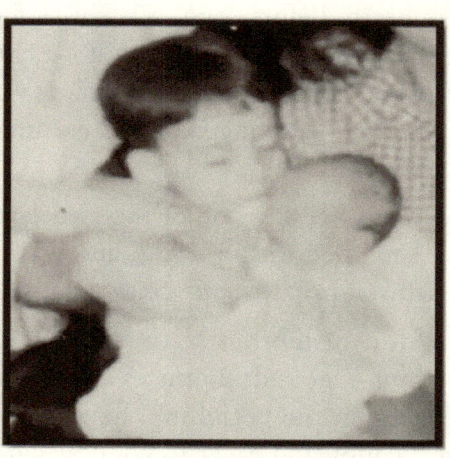

CHAPTER 2

SHAWN ODLE

On October 4, 1977, I became a mother! My baby boy was born healthy, with no signs of any issues. He did have a bit of jaundice and spent his first 24 hours under a light for treatment. At just two weeks old, he developed a severe allergy to disposable diapers, so we switched exclusively to cloth diapers. He was a happy, content baby.

At Shawn's 3-month check-up, I mentioned to the pediatrician that he wasn't holding his head up or gripping anything yet. The doctor brushed off my concerns, reminding me that I was a first-time mom and likely overreacting. He assured me that Shawn appeared healthy in every way.

By the 6-month checkup, I voiced the same concerns again—something just didn't feel right. When the doctor gave me the same dismissive response, I had enough. He had never even taken the time to really examine my baby! I told him that and demanded a referral to Le Bonheur Children's Hospital in Memphis, Tennessee. He hesitated, suggesting we "wait a little longer," but I refused. I told him if he wouldn't refer us, I'd take Shawn myself. That was our last visit to that pediatrician.

From then on, Dr. Edward Ivanić became Shawn's

doctor. Our visit to Le Bonheur didn't reveal any immediate medical issues, but a neurologist diagnosed Shawn with developmental delays, possibly cerebral palsy. Genetic testing showed no abnormalities. We were told there was a 25% chance of recurrence, and that trauma from a previous car accident I was in might have contributed.

Despite his challenges, Shawn grew normally in many ways. He smiled at all the right stages but struggled with motor skills and balance. He commando-crawled around the house, and when he wanted to sit on the couch, he'd pull himself up and scoot into the corner to sit securely. He did the same with corners around the house.

I watched him adapt to his surroundings in incredible ways just so he could play—and he'd laugh with pride when he succeeded. The doctors were often amazed.

At the time, even though I was certified in laboratory technology, I was working at the local shirt factory. Thankfully, our babysitter, Ms. Billie, lived just up the street. She was a gem—she treated Shawn just like the other children, with love and care.

When Shawn was 2 years and 8 months old, his little brother Jason was born. Shawn was thrilled—and so were we. We welcomed Jason with hope and prayers in our hearts.

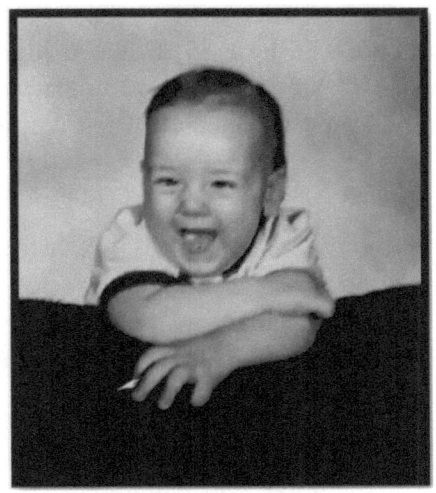

Shawn (The eldest one)

CHAPTER 3

JASON ODLE

Jason was born on June 15, 1977. At just two days old, he lifted his head—strong and full of energy. He was a bundle of pure muscle, and I felt confident that everything was fine. There were no signs of any medical concerns.

When Jason was two months old, we took him along to one of Shawn's appointments at Bonheur. The doctors examined him and said he appeared perfectly healthy, but they wanted to monitor his development over time, just to be sure.

As the months went by, familiar concerns began to surface. The same developmental issues we had seen with Shawn started appearing in Jason. Still, there was no clear diagnosis. Eventually, the doctors began referring to it as cerebral palsy.

Jason (The younger one)

CHAPTER 4

THEIR CHILDHOOD

The two years and eight months I had with Shawn before Jason's birth were filled with a blend of joy, happiness, and struggles.

Shawn began therapy early—starting in October 1975—at the North Mississippi Regional Rehabilitation Center in Tupelo. It was a 68-mile drive each way, and we made the trip two to three times a week. We were also given training and instructions to continue his therapy at home. Shawn truly looked forward to every session, both at the center and at home. He never once complained. He was so full of love and happiness.

Our initial focus was on his physical development. We received a set of exercises to be done daily, some of which required three people to perform. My youngest sister, Valerie, and a step-cousin, Ricky, volunteered to help, and together we committed to the routine every single day.

Jason's arrival brought more joy into our lives, but within a few months, it became clear he too was facing developmental delays. Accepting that reality was devastating. I turned to prayer, and while my faith remained strong, my heart and mind struggled. Still, we began doing the same in-home therapy exercises with Jason that we had used with Shawn. In time, I came to realize that while it was demanding, it was manageable—it just required time and consistency.

Jason eventually began therapy at the same rehabilitation center as Shawn. Both boys quickly became favorites among the therapists, always bringing light and laughter to their sessions.

"All According to God's Plan" became more than just a belief—it was the foundation that carried us through. I was determined to make this journey a successful one, honoring God and glorifying His name every step of the way. And in His goodness, He gave Shawn the perfect companion—his little brother, Jason.

They were inseparable, laughing, playing, and even fighting like typical brothers. I remember one visit when my mother watched them bickering and asked, "Aren't you going to stop them?" I simply replied, "No, not unless I see hair or blood flying. They need to learn how to deal with each other if they're going to get along with anyone else."

They explored the house by commando crawling—dragging themselves across the floor using only their arms. Shawn even taught Jason how to sit up by wedging himself into corners for support. Their favorite spot was the hall closet, so I cleared it out and filled it with toys. Soon, they discovered the kitchen cabinets and would pull out my pots and pans, climb in, and hide from me—though their giggles always gave them away.

Eventually, they graduated from cribs to unstacked bunk beds. They could climb in and out on their own and proudly put themselves to bed. I bought a toy chest that was low enough for them to reach, and they always made sure to clean up after themselves.

One winter, after we'd bought a new refrigerator, they found the giant box it came in. I found them playing inside it, and when I tried to take it away, they cried. Then I had an idea. Our house sat on a hill, so I placed them in the box, climbed in behind them—and off we went sledding down the snowy hill, laughing all the way. We went up and down until my dad stopped by and nearly had a heart attack seeing what I was doing. Oh well!

When Shawn turned four, he started attending the local child development center. The therapists there were wonderful—especially the speech therapist. Jason began at age three and quickly followed in his brother's footsteps. Before they even started formal school, they were already learning colors, shapes, and how to count. The center staff did an amazing job challenging them. This was in the late 1970s and early1980s. Their support gave us strength.

During that time, I returned to college while still working at the shirt factory. I wanted to better understand how to help my sons and others like them reach their full potential.

Church remained a central part of our lives, though not without its challenges. Jason would cry whenever I tried to sing. Still, our faith never wavered. Church was a place of praise, community, and renewal—and without God's love, grace, and guidance, we would've been lost.

But school brought new obstacles. Our county had no appropriate class for physically disabled children. They were classified as such, so our school district contracted with a neighboring county that offered a class at a rehabilitation center.

By the time Shawn started first grade in 1980, I was enrolled at the University of Mississippi (Ole Miss), majoring in clinical psychology with a minor in special education. Our routine was intense: I got both boys ready each morning, Jason caught the bus to the child development center, and I drove Shawn 68 miles to Tupelo for school and therapy. After dropping him off, I drove 50 miles more to attend my classes at Ole Miss. This was our routine for the next two years.

Those daily trips down the Natchez Trace Parkway became our special time. We talked about trees, birds, animals—and always held hands. One day, we saw a squirrel get hit by a car. I stopped, gently placed its seemingly lifeless body in the glove compartment...

only for Shawn to yell, "Mom!" The squirrel was scratching and very much alive! Now imagine!! This wild squirrel is right in front of Shawn! If I opened the glove compartment to release it, it could jump on him. Oh my!

I calmly pulled over, quickly grabbed a blanket to cover Shawn, and released the squirrel without anyone getting hurt. From that moment on—no more wild animal rescues for us!

Shawn's first IEP (Individualized Education Plan) meeting was an eye-opener. The goals were basic—shapes, colors, numbers—but he already knew all of that. When I questioned it, the teacher claimed I was expecting too much. I nearly lost it. She hadn't even given him time to respond properly! When she repeated the assessment in front of me, it became clear: with PMD (Pelizaeus-Merzbacher Disease, as we'd later learn), their brains processed and understood everything—but their bodies responded slowly. It was always easy to see if you looked into their eyes. That was the real challenge of their condition.

Jason started first grade in 1983, joining the same class as Shawn (with different teachers). Thanks to Shawn paving the way, the staff was more prepared. Jason was thrilled to be at school with his big brother.

But during Jason's midterm IEP meeting, something caught my attention. Every day after school, both boys talked non-stop about the soap opera Days of Our Lives. I checked the IEP and saw no challenging goals. When I brought this up, the staff again said, "You're expecting too much. You need to accept their limitations."

I smiled, turned to Shawn, and asked, "What happened on Days of Our Lives today?" He rattled off about Roman and Marlania. The teachers' jaws dropped. It turned out they had been putting all the kids down for naps during that hour—but mine didn't nap. They watched the soap and remembered everything. I said, "If they can remember every character on a soap opera and describe in detail who they are, maybe the issue isn't that I expect too much. Maybe it's that you're not expecting enough." End of discussion. Time to refocus on challenges.

Sharing some very special times with all of you. Not every trip was about getting to school. On our drives, we made nature stops. One of our favorite places was a unique, storm-bent tree along the parkway. It bent just right for the boys to sit on. We talked about how special it was—different for a reason, just like them. God placed that tree there for us, a simple joy in the midst of a busy life. Shawn and Jason loved nature and it's beauty.

Several ask me if they argued and fought. Oh, Heavens Yes—they fought! I carried a rolled-up newspaper while driving just in case I needed to swat at them. Once, they were arguing over a girl in class. Both had motorized wheelchairs by then, and I warned them: "Next time you argue, I'm pulling over and letting you find your way home!" Well, that lasted about five minutes, I did just that—braked, pulled over, and let the lift down. They immediately apologized and begged to stay in the van. It worked! They definitely were typical boys.

Even during summer breaks when school was out, therapy continued. Shawn and Jason also attended summer camps designed for children with special needs.

My senior year at Ole Miss was particularly demanding, and I had to find someone who could pick my guys up and keep them until I arrived. That's when God led us to the Charlie Brown House—a daycare center that also provided after-school services. The staff there were incredible! Shawn and Jason immediately connected with everyone. Not only did the staff care for them, but they also supported their learning and helped with therapy exercises. Truly a blessing from God.

In May of 1984, I graduated from the University of Mississippi with a bachelor's degree in psychology—earning honors. I give all the credit to God and the support system He placed in our lives. The love, joy, and strength I drew from my sons made every long day and sleepless night worth it.

I shared that special graduation day with them, and with my older sister and her husband, who lovingly brought the boys so they could be part of the celebration.

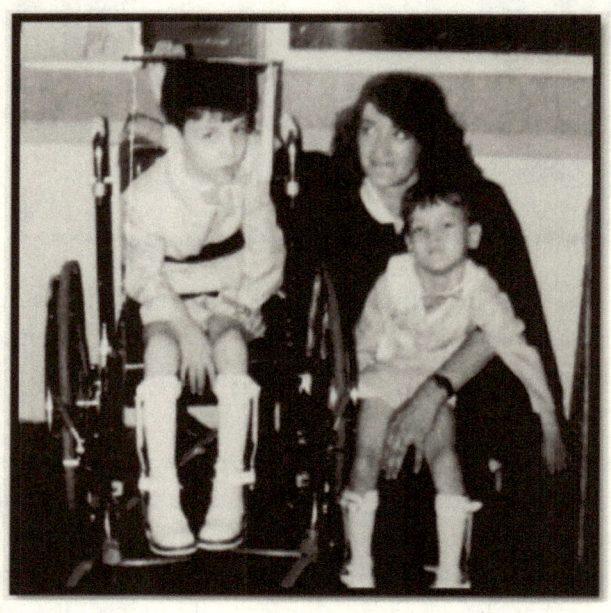

That summer, I began working under the guidance of a psychologist and a psychiatrist at North Mississippi Medical Center in Tupelo. The opportunity provided valuable hands-on experience and helped prepare me for the next step—entering the doctoral program in clinical psychology.

CHAPTER 5

OUR FAITH IN GOD

From the very beginning, God and the church have been at the center of our family. Not once did I ask, "Why?" My faith never wavered. I trusted completely in God's purpose for my sons—and in my own purpose as their mother. I knew He was watching over us.

Each day began with praise-filled prayers, grace was said over every meal, and bedtime always ended with prayers for rest and protection. I read Bible stories from children's books to Shawn and Jason.

A kind woman from our church would visit occasionally to read to them as well. Their faces would light up with joy at hearing God's Word, and they eagerly answered every question she asked afterward. They learned the hymns by heart, even if they couldn't always sing along. At home, we took our time—I'd sing part of a hymn, and they'd finish it. We did the same with Bible verses, giving them the space they needed to respond.

The world outside often moved too fast to notice the depth of their understanding, but I saw it every day. My heart soared the day Shawn told me he wanted to be a preacher. While others may have seen that as impossible, I knew his life alone would be his ministry.

As our story unfolds in this series called Hearts of Gold, you'll witness the miracles of how God worked through both Shawn and Jason.

"Greater is He that is in me than he that is in the world!"

1 John 4:4

"I am more than a conqueror."

Romans 8:37

"I am above only and not beneath."

Duet. 28:13

"I am blessed coming in and blessed going out."

Duet. 28:6

"If God is for me, who can be against me?!"

Romans 8:31

SEE YOURSELF HOW GOD SEES YOU

You are a masterpiece, a new creation, filled with the very Spirit of God. You are valuable, worthy, and capable of extraordinary things. No force can stop you from God's Plan for your life. Your future is bright.

CHAPTER 6

GOD'S PLAN: ADVOCATES FOR CHANGE

For I know the plans I have for you," declares the Lord, "plans to prosper you and not to harm you, plans to give you hope and a future."

Jeremiah 29:11

In the Fall of 1985 our school district began a class for students with varying disabilities. Shawn and Jason began classes at Marietta Elementary School located only 5 miles from home. The teacher was open minded and prepared to challenge them. They enjoyed being with other non-disabled children their age. They enjoyed watching the games being played and participating as much as possible in them. It was at that time I realized the gift of joy God had placed in their hearts. Although they weren't able to actively participate they enjoyed watching the other children. They were a joy and blessing to everyone.

With this class also came a camaraderie with other parents of children with special needs. We formed a group called North Mississippi Coalition of Citizens with Disabilities. It was not only a parent group but one which included all ages. There had never been such a group for our area. It grew fast and expanded beyond our expectations. Soon we were being invited by our local legislators to testify at the state Capitol. With gaining notoriety we were also approached by agency directors to attend board meetings. This lead to Children's Medical Program of the Mississippi State Department of Health requesting assistance in forming a parent advisory board for its program. This was the beginning of the bigger plan God had. Within a year we were being requested by the US Surgeon General C. Everett Koop to attend a meeting and give testimony on the need for community-based services for children with disabilities. This trip would include all the professionals involved with Shawn and Jason because we had built a team at the community level that proved the benefits of community-based services. They're pediatrician, teacher, and after school provider.

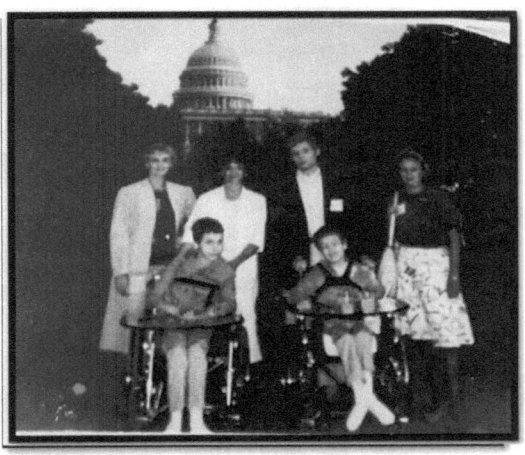

What began as a grassroots effort soon grew into legislative action and nationwide advocacy aimed at improving the lives of people with disabilities.

The path to advocacy was filled with friendships—some lasting, some fading as our journey progressed. Yet each one remains cherished in our hearts. From our humble beginnings as a small parent-led group in northeast Mississippi, we found ourselves on the national stage, where I had the honor of serving as a keynote speaker for the U.S. Surgeon General.

Words can hardly capture the depth of love, support, and unwavering faith that carried us through these milestones. What we achieved was never ours alone—it was part of something greater. We know, without a doubt, it was God's plan from the very beginning.

Two little boys, born to a country girl, would rise through their challenges to help spark meaningful change in health care, education, and social services—paving the way for future generations.

Public Law (PL) 94-142, also known as the Education for All Handicapped Children Act (EHA) or the Individuals with Disabilities Education Act (IDEA), is a federal law that guarantees free and appropriate public education (FAPE) for children with disabilities, was passed by the US Congress the year Shawn was born 1974. It would be years before this law would be appropriately carried out in local school districts. It would take parents being educated and aware of their children's right in order to fully implement that law. To this day there's an ongoing effort for parent training and information in every state. PL 94-142 was the origin of the law that many educators now known as the Individuals with Disabilities Education Act (IDEA). Foundational to students receiving a Free Appropriate Public Education (FAPE), PL 94-142 has aided schools in providing equal access to education for over 7.5 million children with disabilities.

The Individuals with Disabilities Education Act (IDEA) was passed in 1986 to authorize early intervention services for infants and toddlers with disabilities:

Part C: Focuses on early intervention services for children from birth to age 3

Part B, Section 619: Authorizes grants to states for preschool programs for children ages 3 through 5

IDEA ensures that states and public agencies provide early intervention, special education, and related services to eligible children and youth with disabilities.

The Home and Community-Based Services (HCBS) waiver program was established by the Omnibus Budget Reconciliation Act of 1981 and incorporated into the Social Security Act at Section 1915(c).

The HCBS waiver program allows states to provide a variety of services under Medicaid as an alternative to institutional care. The waiver made it possible availability to all regard of income or resources.

Although passed in 1981 few states had chosen to buy into this option. The general public including

those in need of these services were unaware of the provisional act.

Home of Your Own Initiative was started as an effort to assist individuals with disabilities who desire a home to be able to achieve their dream. It would require teams of individuals working with the person in order to successfully achieve this. Shawn and Jason were the first homeowners with disabilities in our home state of Mississippi. Through the efforts of staff of University of Southern Mississippi's Institution for Disability Studies (IDS), individuals with disabilities and parents this program succeeded in assisting many to achieve their dreams of homeownership.

Managing various diagnoses with no conclusive evidence left us not knowing what we were dealing with. From cerebral palsy to neuroaxonal dystrophy but never anything definitive.

My final decision, after numerous tests and studies some which were painful, was they were my sons and that's all that mattered. I was going to give them the best life I possibly could.

It was only after years of involvement in the field of disability that I became acquainted with someone doing genetic research. She requested to include Shawn and Jason in her studies. It was at that time in 1995 that we got a definite diagnosis. Pelizaeus–Merzbacher disease (PMD) is a rare genetic disorder that affects the central nervous system and is linked to problems with the white matter of the brain and spinal cord. It is classified as a leukodystrophy, meaning it involves abnormal development of the myelin sheath, the protective covering of nerves. The myelin sheath is essential for normal nerve function, and without it, nerves cannot work properly. In PMD, different areas of the central nervous system are impacted, including deep parts of the brain (subcortical), cerebellum (which helps with movement coordination, brain stem (which controls vital functions) and spinal cord. The main symptoms of PMD include difficulty coordinating movement (ataxia), involuntary muscle spasms (spasticity), leading to stiff and slow leg movements, delays in reaching developmental milestones (e.g., sitting, walking), loss of motor abilities later in life and progressive intellectual decline. PMD is caused by changes (variants) in the PLP1 gene. Several forms of PMD have been identified, including: -Classic PMD-Con-natal PMD (present at birth) -Transitional PMD PLP1 null syndrome (no PLP1 protein produced)-Other related conditions caused by PLP1 gene variants include complicated spastic paraparesis, pure spastic paraparesis (SPG2) and hypomyelination of early myelinating structures (HEMS). The disease usually progresses slowly, with worsening neurological symptoms over time. Treatment is based upon the specific symptoms that the affected person may have. Source: National Organization of Rare Disorders (NORD). While the diagnosis was a bit disturbing it gave a comforting sense of finally knowing. This answered many questions surrounding their difficulties but it didn't change who they had become despite their challenges. They were two amazing young men as you will read about in the following series of books.

TESTIMONIALS:

Julie Baker After school care: 1984

Time with Shawn and Jason has been a blessing filled with insights into their world as they freely engaged as much as possible in activities with other children. When they couldn't engage in the activities they enjoyed watching, laughing and cheer the others on. It was an amazing delight to see such joy come from them. Their attitudes are so positive. I believe that comes from their mother's acceptance and expectations regardless of their limitations. She treats them as if they are normal as others.

Billie Norris child care: 1975-1980

Shawn just fit right in with the other children even though he was unable to keep up with them. The children were so great with him, brining toys and sharing crayons to color. They are all such a blessing to watch. Untouched by social expectations and judgment of what's normal. Then here comes Jason. They are brothers but so different in personalities. Jason's mom still breast feeds and comes everyday during her lunch break to breastfeed him. He's definitely a moma's boy. He's very outgoing and gets into anything within his reach. He loves to explore which he does by rolling. Shawn is the quiet one. He studies everyone. He watches and waits for his opportunity to engage. He too rolls but also commando crawls to get to places. There're 2 steps going from the kitchen into the activity room. I almost panicked one day when I saw Shawn in the kitchen!! He had climbed the steps crawling. A gate was immediately installed. Oh, these boys!! I will never put anything past them. Mom is the instigator because she encourages their explorations limiting them only for safety. Kathy is as special as they are.

Teacher
Martha Cartwright 1985-87

As this school year began I took the position at Marietta Elementary School for the newly created classroom for special needs children. It was a class of four initially. My first day I meet the parents and students. Two young boys were brothers and their mom had many expectations. I really wasn't sure of myself to be able to accomplish such tasks because of their severe limitations. It didn't take long for mom and these guys to teach me about adaptations. I had read their records from the Tupelo City School system but it nowhere prepared me for the challenge ahead of me. I must say they challenged me more than I challenged them. I learned from them and their mom everyday to be open minded and never say Can't be done. Of course, it couldn't be done the conventional way but these guys were anything except conventional. And with a strong advocate such as mom I was sure they would make changes in conventional ways of thinking. To Kathy, their mom, there were no limits until proven. She had accepted their mobility would be via wheelchair and had insisted with doctors to get motorized wheelchairs. Who am I to say No to such a strong-willed mom.

As more students were added the second year these three moms created a parent group which later grew into a coalition of parents and individuals with disabilities. As I worked with these very special children, I also observed their very special parents. My entire outlook on life was changed. My faith in God was strengthened as I saw with God anything is possible.

Speech therapist 1979-1987

Shawn and Jason are such a delight to work with: So is their highly motivating mother. At the beginning of therapy, I was working together with them. But very quickly I separated them and only engaged them together at the end. Shawn was dominating the sessions. Kathy, their mom, had cautioned me on that. She was right!! Kathy also desired the guys have a communication device. I will recommend that to their doctor. At this point I believe it would facilitate their communication not to replace verbal communication. These guys are very verbal. The only difficulty is the patience of the listeners. Their speech is labored and requires good listening skills. They are both very patient with repeating themselves if they perceive someone is truly listening. Otherwise, you will get ignored by them. They are very in tune with if you are actively listening to them. They also give environmental cues very well such as pointing. Their level of understanding is not impaired.

It's clear in their eyes however due to neuromuscular limitations it takes a bit of time to respond verbally.

The new communication devise has been received. Shawn was very interested in learning it but Jason seems to think it's a toy. Pictures, signs and letters are incorporated into the devise. It only took a few sessions until Shawn understood the use of the devise. Jason did well but still treats it like a toy.

Over the eight years working with these brothers, I've seen so much progress. Their speech improved into complete sentences and no longer need the devise. They challenge each other in all aspects and have been amazing to work with.

Family member Aunt Sue Nell

My memory takes me back to the time I kept Shawn and Jason while Kathy was in the hospital. Shawn was perfectly happy and enjoying himself. He loved sitting with my husband Norman and listening to the CB radio. Jason was breastfed and not yet weaned. He cried for 2 nights and days. Nothing would pacify him but his mama. He was rocked to sleep but would wake up crying. My heart broke for his sweet little heart. Kathy was hospitalized for a week by that time Jason had adjusted to the bottle. He was playing and enjoying his time with us. They enjoyed their cousins but especially enjoyed their Pawpaw and Nanny Odle. Shawn watches over his baby brother. The love these two have is heartwarming. These sweet special nephews have my heart and so do their mother. It is easy to see God is with them.

Aunt Valerie. Kathy's sister

As we traveled along... Shawn and Jason what a pair. My sister's total joy in life. I had the joy of learning the ins and outs of hands in Physical Therapy with my nephews. Each week I would ride my bike to my sister's home. At the onset as my sister would guide me through the movements Fear set in. I was so afraid of hurting them. As a teen I was not aware of the benefits the physical therapy was providing to each of them. My sister Kathy would spur me along to be more firm in the therapy process. The boys were already independent as they could be. They found a way to get from point A to point B much quicker than one would ever expect. Shawn was always a bit more outspoken but they didn't have to speak for me to see the love on their faces each time I arrived. A few years later a need arose for a driver to take the boys to their therapy center in Tupelo MS. I had to pleasure of being that driver. Each trip we loaded up my son who was less than a year old with Shawn and brother Jason.

Shawn and Jason loved my son. However, they panicked if he ever cried. Both boys would not settle until my son was soothed.

Now in the car it was Shawn or Jason shotgun in front with me and my son in car seat in back. I tried to switch them out as to who could ride next to my son.

If Shawn was in the back seat, he would reach his hand over and hold the car seat.

We would try our best to enjoy our 35-40 minute ride. Along our way we would at times make a stop at my in-laws.

My mother-in-law was always fascinated with Shawn and Jason's independence.

She always wanted to help them with everything. But as it turned out she learned that both boys were in less need of assistance than she thought.

The years went by and the boys aged as did we all I remained amazed at the accomplishments the boys made each year. Their resilience, courage and love for all in their lives is what carried them into manhood. A true example of perseverance.

Not to mention a mother who guided, guarded and protected them.

Shawn and Jason, My whole family has a special place in our hearts for you both.

We miss you.

ABOUT THE AUTHOR

"Kathy Pounds Graham is a pioneer in the fight for Equality in the Field of Disabilities. She had a vision that her sons & others would have the same opportunities in life their able-bodied peers enjoyed."

Because of her vision, dedication, determination and faith in God, many opportunities for people with disabilities were created. Many of these opportunities she and her sons planted seeds for have come to fruition and allow people to live, work, recreate and participate in life next to their peers. Although her sons are no longer with us Kathy continues the legacy she and her sons began in 1974. She continues to educate the public about the world of disabilities Through. The Eyes of she and her sons as they made history. "Submitted by Vicki Killingsworth, Master's degree in education, fellow advocate and coworker.

Kathy is the proud mother of two young men born with a rare disorder limiting their abilities to live life as society dictates. She became a warrior in the fight for her sons' rights to live as normal a life as possible as well as all children similar to them. She taught her sons to speak up and advocate as well.

Anonymously submitted.

She is also a warrior in her faith and belief that Jesus Christ is the son of the living God and he came to earth to die on the cross for humankind's remission of sins. A woman strong in her faith and humble to her Lord and Savior. This will be evident throughout the pages of testimony in this documentary of her sons' lives entitled Hearts of Gold: Broken Bodies, Immeasurable Blessings.

the pages of testimony in this documentary of her sons' lives entitled Hearts of Gold: Broken Bodies, Immeasurable Blessings.